WHAT TODAY'S PARENT **MUST** KNOW ABOUT TODAY'S CLASSROOM

MEETING THE CHALLENGE OF NEW AGE LEARNERS

KENDRICK S. STERLING

Charleston, SC
www.PalmettoPublishing.com

What Today's Parent Must *Know About Today's Classroom*
Copyright © 2021 by Kendrick S. Sterling

First Edition

Hardcover ISBN: 978-1-63837-698-9
Paperback ISBN: 978-1-63837-699-6
eBook ISBN: 978-1-63837-961-4

CONTENTS

INTRODUCTION

Dear Parents,

The information that I long to share with you is life changing for anyone in or around education today; students, teachers, administrators and even entire school communities. However, I would like to be very clear - you, the parents are my primary motivation and drive for sharing what I have learned. So, to all whom may be a part of any recently stated populations...I ask for your forgiveness in advance and request humbly of you to wear your parent hat or put yourself in the place of today's parents working with a forever growing and changing school society.

I'm there early when you pull up. It's dark and you may not be fully awake but you show great appreciation for the extended day program that allows you to have a secure dwelling for your child/children before the school opens and helps you prepare for work in time. I'm putting up the flag, but I see you.

I'm there when you surprise your scholar at lunch and get to experience the pure joy of a child elated to see you. You still have your work clothes on, badge and all, but you make time for your child and create memories that either of you won't soon forget. The children talk about it for weeks! I'm on lunch or recess duty, but I see you.

I'm there when you arrive at dismissal and you and your beloved child/children are spent from the days' events/activities and you remind each other that it's time for family, rest and relaxation. The indescribable joy between parent and child is one that I have been privileged to see day in and day out for 20 years. I'm on car rider...or bus...or walker duty, but I see you.

The thought of a single child missing out on the amazing educational experiences offered in today's schools such as songs, games, poetry, interactive technology, and cooperative learning groups, just to name a few, is shameful! I aim to reach as many families and classrooms as possible because our children can't afford a year, a month, a week, a day, an hour, or a minute receiving instruction that is less than amazing. Today's classrooms are amazing and its time everyone knows!

"Mr. Sterling...What have you done with this child? He was in my office quite a bit in previous school years." I have heard it repeatedly. "It must be because you are a man" is what many have said. The secret...I love them like they are my own because they have been entrusted to me and I believe to teach is a calling. I don't believe any child was placed in my care accidentally. My students know they are loved and can make mistakes. Period.

Throughout the text, I intend to highlight the wonders that make up today's classrooms and invite the parent to be fully engulfed by the experience. As educators we are all too familiar with your feelings of hopelessness and/or anger with a system that does not always seem to make complete and total sense. To my educators, looking for ways to work smarter and not harder...stick around! You equally motivate me as I observe your daily grind and dedication to educate students of all learning levels.

There will be common themes shared throughout the text such as "responsibility of all"; parent, student, and teacher. Each "must" will be featured and its importance for all learners; relationships, learning groups, note booking, centers/stations, technology, and movement. The 5E model of instruction along with the three levels of learners most teachers plan and implement instruction for daily/weekly will be clearly explained. The three main types of learners; audio, visual, kinesthetic will be addressed to help parents better identify "how their children enjoy learning".

One of the latest influences that I aim to share with parents, students, and educators are the "Seven Habits of Highly Effective People" by Stephen R. Covey, New York Times Bestselling Author. The habits are "Be Proactive",

"Begin with the End in Mind", "Put First Things First", "Think Win-Win", "Seek First to Understand Then to Be Understood", "Synergize", and "Sharpen the Saw". The habits have been adjusted to fit the needs of all elementary level learners and leaders are being identified and celebrated through our school's "Leader in Me!" program. The habits have been instrumental to the lives of all involved. The growth and development of young scholars in our community has been evident.

I would like to credit the institutions that assisted me in my own growth and development. MacGregor E.S., Edward H. White E.S., Sharpstown M.S., Sharpstown H.S. and Houston Baptist University.

To each school I am eternally grateful. My early childhood consisted of Tchaikovsky, Bach, Shakespeare and other classics while many of my peers faced issues of drugs, gangs and senseless violence. Culture and self-determination were both modeled for me early in life and today's children deserve the same. Today's parent must know of all the incredible experiences that take place daily in effective classrooms. This knowledge will inspire parents worldwide to insist all children have access to these experiences!

I will not dismiss the role of the child and the family because I was taught by respected veteran teachers that the first teacher in any student's life is in the home; instructing, guiding, and providing immediate feedback about what is acceptable or not. However, my intent is to share with parents the latest tested and proven strategies on how to best educate today's learner while mastering today's evolving curriculum.

Since I began teaching in 2000 I have been told "parents are a variable we cannot control". I believe if we are working in true partnership with families "control" is not an issue to be discussed. We are creating "leaders who are in control of their own learning". Informed parents make quality schools because they refuse to accept anything less than the best for their children. Parents who are not "caught up" on the latest techniques in the classroom can do more harm than good, even though their intentions are quite the opposite.

In my now 20 year assessment of teachers and learners, I have learned not all of today's educators feel it is necessary to study and/or apply today's best teaching methods once the doors to the classroom are closed. These choices are affecting directly the growth and development of children and their communities are suffering as result. Education is too important to any community and its future to possess anything less than a highly effective teacher. Parents this is your right!

All teachers must attend professional development yearly. However, the application of new techniques/strategies can sometimes be frowned upon by the educator because "it is not how they learned". If parents are equipped with best practices that have proven success, they can now inquire as to why these practices may be absent in some classrooms and/or schools. Many families are struggling to "connect" with their children and their educational development because they just don't know the latest effective methods administered regularly with success.

The classroom has been transformed from a "teacher-centered" environment to a "student-centered" environment. We no longer establish goals to pass a test, but instead aim to create lifelong learners. The goal is to create scholars whom understand that they have a purpose and commitment to community. Instructed through a "growth mindset" today's student is challenged to ponder how they will best benefit the family, the community and themselves. We need our parents to make a paradigm shift as well, grasping the change in style and allow today's student to learn through discovery and exploration. Humans are naturally inquisitive and the best teachers use this knowledge to excite learners daily!

There are tangible reasons children get excited for some learning environments and loathe others. Something is missing and with love for the children guiding us...we can create the greatest classrooms for all children. I believe in my heart of hearts that if I asked any parent a simple question, they would all say yes.

"Would you be interested in proven techniques/ strategies ensuring your scholar will love school and schoolwork while erasing issues with discipline and/or focus?"

It is time for teachers to stand on their desks and parents to stand at the front door demanding we make every school in America the best it can be. The time is now. Our children are our greatest resource, but if we don't see the value of each student, an immeasurable price will be paid. Learning, growth, and mastery happens when parents, teachers and schools put children first and combine to have one force moving in the same direction…forward!

BUILDING RELATIONSHIPS

*To make a connection to; involvement

*Emotional or other connection
between teacher and family

Building relationships is the most important "must" of the six to be discussed. Without quality relationships built on trust, students can never reach their full potential. Developing strong positive relationships with children and being excited about their growth and development is the very purpose of becoming an educator. We ask children to take risk, dive into the unknown and trust that we will be there when they stumble. We tell them a slight nudge is coming and that you might fall and may experience some pain in the process. We tell them we will guide them to safe havens if they need to be "retaught" and that they should fear not because we are present. When this trust is lost or broken between the student, the teacher and the parent, the damage can be horrific.

So, nothing much I advise after this point will matter if every parent and teacher of record does not choose to love whole-heartedly every single student that they are entrusted to. My insight is derived from 20 years of "August to June!" Children make you earn their trust and admiration and rightly so. As parents, maybe that is a lesson for us also. I credit my knowledge as well to the many veteran teachers that invested time in me when I had very sincere questions about my attempts to "reach a student" by any means necessary. They spoke the truth in me and they spoke in love.

That was the key. "Love the kids, prepare and plan for all of them, invest your time and resources in them and more than all that, respect each and every child." This, and many other statements, led me to think about a few students that had shown growth or had struggled due to good or bad relationships with teachers. I witnessed personally how the power of love can transform a child and I knew from then on, it was the only way to effectively educate.

Effective educators have a very clear understanding of their place in every student's life. They consider it honor and privilege to spend their years modeling, guiding, and caring for students. Most will tell you it doesn't feel like work because they love what they do so much. But trust me, there is no tired like teacher tired! Each new student is an opportunity to display the skills and training teachers are blessed to gain and develop. A new student is never seen as a burden. One thousand four hundred forty (1,440) hours a year is roughly the amount of time your child spends yearly in school! (180 days times 8 hours/8,640 hours K-5) The lack of a quality relationship between the parent, teacher and student can be, and often is devastating.

For example, let me tell you about "Kevin and Shane". Kevin, a 5th grader that could be found in any major city in America, was often described as hyper or quite active, to say the least. He was the student that many of us are warned about in professional development courses. Unfortunately, he was also the student that some teachers discuss in private, condemning him before providing him an opportunity to flourish. His "performances" preceded him and along with this reputation came a different set of expectations. To be quite honest, this student was me.

Now Kevin is on my class list and I began to hear the whispers. "So, Mr. Sterling, I heard you were getting our friend Kevin this year." I would always respond in kind. "Kevin will get Mr. Sterling this year and I look forward to seeing his growth and development!" I have always relished the opportunity to assist young scholars upon their path to do the impossible. To invest time, love, and energy into children that may be lacking in one or all those areas is the foundation for educating. What a teacher gets to witness yearly each spring, after planting and nurturing seeds all fall to winter, is nothing short of amazing! I was excited to have Kevin in my class and I immediately attached his success that year to my own. If he failed, it would be because my efforts failed him.

My initial goal was to make this young man shine for all to see, but mostly for him to see the light in himself! I wanted him to see that he could do things he didn't previously believe he could. We accomplished that goal in the first few weeks of school. It wasn't always easy but it was always rewarding for him and me both. Kevin and I made a deal. The goal was to send home a daily report that would make his family proud. When Kevin needed a reminder, I would simply remind him of his power to affect the mood of his home. He bought in to my request and he started to see positive outcomes in class and at home.

To be quite honest the first weeks of school are always challenging because new routines and expectations are being set between the teacher, the student and the family. When Kevin spoke out of turn or made poor choices, he had to be disciplined with love and reminded of the rules. He had to be reminded why it was paramount that I have his full attention during class. "Kevin, throughout the week I am sharing with you the knowledge that will help you pass my test! Don't you want to do well?" He always said yes and during times of instruction he always knew I would involve him. I always assured him that he would have opportunities to discuss learning objectives with his peers.

We call this "Think, Turn and Talk". Students get excited about new information and must have a minute or so (30-60 seconds is more than enough time) to discuss these topics with their peers. This strategy allows young scholars to connect new information with background knowledge. Kevin was never disobedient when he had an opportunity to speak out and share. He became quite the gentleman and did not disturb instruction time. He knew that he would always have a chance to speak and he also knew that his teacher would be excited to hear him and whatever information he decided to share. He agreed to the terms we both set and Kevin and I got off to a great start. I learned through this child the power of quality relationships and how anything less than genuine love, honor, and respect could be devastating for a young learner.

Kevin displayed difficulty making new friends early in the school year. He did have a bit of a reputation from previous years. I assured him that in time he could renew his relationships with his peers but he would have to trust me and be patient in his attempts. Just as he was learning to become trustworthy, he was also learning that only trust could repair poor decision making amongst his peers. I shared with him many of the hot topics that students discussed at recess and/or lunch and how he could become a part of the discussion without "bullying his way in." He started to make friends right away.

The children started to see what I saw in him. He was a pleasant young man whom had been through some very unpleasant circumstances. His emotional backpack was full and he struggled with processing his emotions. I was also making a new friend, and he knew I truly cared about him. Kevin felt important because he was a part of the process and what he felt mattered. He was invited to be a part of his educational development instead of being told he had to conform to "my" class. He knew it was "our" class and that he was very special to the teacher, everyday!

Kevin went on to have an outstanding school year. He blew away his past performances on the state test and made more growth that year than all other students in my class. I believe this happened because he started to believe in himself and knew Mr. Sterling would catch him if he fell down. I even suggested that this young man be screened for the district's Gifted and Talented program. He proved that he could not only learn but excel and displayed very unique ways of thinking about and presenting mastered content.

Unfortunately, I saw him began to go backwards the following year because some of his middle school teachers would rely on his reputation versus the quality young man we all saw leaving my classroom with pride and dignity. Kevin, in just a few months into the new school year, was being sent out of class. He was frustrated, angry and searching for love and while outside that room he was learning nothing good to aid his development. I hated the reports I received from administrators and I felt his pain. I had wished that all his teachers might invest in the extra time and energy needed to support a child like him, but I was reminded of our first few weeks together. Kevin could be very difficult if he didn't feel safe and welcomed.

Then there was "Shane". This wonderfully unique child tested every ounce of my knowledge towards assisting neglected and/or abused children. And every bit of my patience. He was an extremely defiant and mean-spirited child. It was clear he was hurting and he let anyone within range know about it. The world was not a loving place for Shane. How could he be expected to have love for others? To make him even more delightful, he was skilled in the art of "recruiting" other scarred children to join him in making very poor choices in and out of school. Shane's poor self-image and behavior affected his ability to learn and severely hurt his growth and development as an emergent reader.

Other teachers would say, "Maybe you will be good for this student." I believed and claimed that statement and took it as a personal challenge to transform Shane into a student that would grow to love learning and excel in school. Just as I did with Kevin, I immediately attached his success that year to my own. If he failed. it would be because my efforts failed him. I admit, not every teacher will subscribe to such a statement, but if you don't truly believe you are equipped to transform the lives of children, what's the purpose?

I would adjust every lesson I taught to make sure that he, and any other struggling students, would feel value and grow from their points of origin. Educators today are expected to prepare lessons that address the needs of learners on level, above level, and below level. Every parent, just as Shane's parents learned, must work alongside the educator to ensure that measured growth is taking place. Quick checks provide valuable data and should drive regular instruction, as well as "prescriptive homework". Small groups allow teachers discrete opportunities to clear misconceptions and answer questions students may not ask in whole group settings. This is where trust abounds!

Shane was seeing himself in a new light and I believe he enjoyed the extra attention and care.

I'm not afraid to admit that some of the stories I'd heard about Shane caused me to wonder how much truth was in the legend. I had some doubt that maybe what worked in the past may not be suitable in this relationship. However, I trusted my heart and the methods I studied in preparation for Shane before I even knew him. To reform a hurting child is extra work, some early mornings and late evenings, but all effective teachers know the return on investment is so awesome we continue to sign up to do it again year after year! I found out what many educators before me knew already… love always works!

The welfare of the children near Shane was also a concern. There was a history of violence and I needed this young man to feel love and respect. My day became more challenging due to the amount of personal attention and direct instruction Shane needed. I promised him I would always be there to assist him in his efforts and he took me up on my offer…at every opportunity. Small group workstations allowed me to assist Shane regularly and really get to know who he was and how enjoyed learning! He appreciated an inviting and effective routine that he found comfort in. Shane started to excel and we were both relieved.

He had a decent year, I expected a commended performance, yet he passed the mandated state tests necessary to move on to the next grade level. His effort proved to be satisfactory for us both. Greater than that was the lifestyle change that took place that year. This was now a student who understood the reasoning and purpose behind studying and being proactive. He had the grades to support his new beliefs and the amount of parental and/or administrative assistance needed for discipline issues in the classroom decreased to none!

Shane still made mistakes from time to time and I was always there to lovingly remind him of the guidelines and expectations we set together. I told him "greatness lies within"…because that was taught to me and this young man, like Kevin, started to see it and believe it. The growth, both academically and socially, these young men made in a year's time was nothing short of astonishing. I'm extremely grateful for the opportunity to develop young minds and develop classrooms filled with love and respect.

Once again, I saw a student move on to the next grade level and began to lose that joy of learning he had gained. Shane started experiencing an abundance of quiet time to reflect outside his classroom and usually this means there are issues inside the classroom. I approached him and inquired as to what we could do to ensure he is in class learning and not spending so much time reflecting. His words broke my heart, "We don't get to move around in here and I liked school better when I was in your classroom."

Of course, it was the freedom that Shane spoke of that he missed. He missed the opportunities to explore and make mistakes without being judged or ridiculed. He missed the responsibility of getting necessary resources in class independently. He didn't feel safe enough to take risks in class and his deficiencies were more on display than his strengths. He shared his wish to have a classroom similar to the one we had both created and I felt his pain. This child was losing his love for learning.

Shane could have been just as successful as he was in my class if some of the effective strategies implemented would have continued. There should have been a meeting to discuss what worked for this student previously and what services we had available as the family's school of choice. That meeting never took place but I assisted the family where I could.

I love teaching, and I love the time, energy, and resources the job demands. We have all been asked to adjust our teaching styles from the very ways that most of us learned. The best teachers know the rewards far outnumber the long days and hard nights. So many teachers step up to the challenges awaiting them daily. The most effective teachers continue to learn and grow with the children they are facilitating. Every classroom in every school deserves "that" teacher!

The classroom has moved from a "teacher-centered" environment to one that is completely "student-centered". Many of us remember "sit and get" – not the most enjoyable or effective way of instructing young scholars. Many parents are not aware that today's average 8-10 year-old students are giving small group PowerPoint presentations with their peers and loving it! Today's scholars have options as to how they represent knowledge gained. Product menus provide students a variety of options from game boards, songs, and poetry to enhanced comic book designs all exhibiting that student's mastery of the content.

I truly want to believe that all teachers love children the way I do. I want to believe that all teachers work long hours at home and explore new ways to make the classroom a wonder each and every day. I want to believe that all teachers learn awesome new things in professional development courses and ignite a passion for learners upon returning to the classroom. Unfortunately, this is not the case in every classroom and for every student. This is where a well-informed parent can build a quality and loving relationship with the teacher. The parent should know what methods/techniques work best for their scholars and teacher should want to work in partnership with parents who will make their work "smarter and not harder".

Effective educators have grasped new ideas and methods of instruction that today's students are excited about. Today's classroom must have a regular and routine use of technology, interactive note booking, cooperative learning groups as well as many other strategies and techniques provided us. Principals and other educators sometimes inquire as to how some teachers are extremely successful with all learners and others struggle. I attribute any and all success effective educators have to building relationships with children and families. It's why we put in the extra time. We work with the most precious of resources.

The time has come that every parent knows of these methods and make them readily available to all children. Every parent must work in unison with today's teachers and ensure that the best available proven and effective methods of instruction are happening daily. Our children are worth it. Every child deserves a highly effective teacher that wants to see every child succeed. Preparing scholars for the next level drives instruction and planning. Classwork/homework have become more prescriptive and today's scholars are getting their needs met in a more personalized manner.

A very wise veteran teacher once told me "No one has all the answers, if they did, we would be doing it" and I wholeheartedly agree. One thing I know for sure is the relationship between the parent and their school of choice is monumental in the growth and development of every scholar. A well-informed parent can ensure a quality education for their child/children through minimal efforts. Parents that are uninterested in the daily and weekly educational lives of their scholar(s) will soon produce a child or children that become uninterested in school. Clear and concise communication with teachers and school administrators can make school a joyful and purposeful process.

Teachers need to teach from their hearts and meet learners where they are. Children know real love. Parents know real love. Both parties will and should explore opportunities early in the school year to know what type of relationship teachers aim to achieve. Effective teachers love children as if they are their own. Planting seeds of love, patience, and kindness is what we do daily. It's all worth it to see a child in the Spring that has begun to love him/herself and the tasks associated with studying, learning, and growing.

It is the parents place to teach children love of self and respect for others before coming to school. The parent must ensure that their child respects teachers and the learning process. Equally, every parent has the right and duty to ensure that the teacher respects the child and all invested family members. Only through a quality partnership with open lines of communication can we produce the type of scholars we are aiming for!

Parents, this means staying aware of the latest instructional techniques your student(s) may explore daily/weekly. Teachers this means sharing with all parents; success stories in class, technology students are excited about, and guided/modeling methods that prove to be affective for the students. A simple email, phone call, and/or conversation during a planned visit will do the trick and goes a long way towards helping each child reach their full potential.

Teachers and parents should share one common goal. Identify student strengths and growth opportunities in relation to their mastery of the intended curriculum. Once this information is provided, we must spend every educational opportunity to strengthen identified areas of weakness. Today's education has become more prescriptive and today's schools are taking a more targeted approach to learning. Effective educators are excited about the next opportunity to develop a student and help them see their full potential. We aim to be a part of the reason these scholars grow strong in multiple areas of instruction.

Educators understand the many types of learners that may enter our classrooms. Auditory learners attain information best through back and forth conversation as they connect new information to background knowledge. A song or poem may also be a chosen method for auditory learners. Visual learners attain information best through sight. Visual aids such as picture vocabulary and guided video animation excite these learners. Kinesthetic learners are hands on. These children learn best through manipulating materials designed to help the learner feel a connection to problem solving. These children require hands on science and/or simulated technology that motivates them to discover through exploration.

Every child has a bit of all three types, however many lean towards one type or the other. Educators must provide a variety of instructional methods including songs, videos, art, student-led presentations, journaling, as well as many others. It is vital that parents know and understand the methods in which their child(ren) enjoy learning. If teachers and parents are not aware of the latest proven methods of instruction, children become bored with learning and all parties are unlikely to see progress and desired outcomes achieved.

Parents play the most important role in the educational development of their children. They are the first teacher. However, working in partnership with teachers and school administrators can guarantee success if all parties are completely involved. Educators have been provided the unique opportunity to provide love, hope, guidance and caring instruction through productive routines. Parents must be a regular part of the process. We simply cannot do it alone and neither party should have to.

Building quality relationships between families and schools is by far the most important aspect of educating today's child. All other topics discussed will not have much validity or reliability if a strong partnership is not formed. Daily parenting demands alongside the many demands of today's educators require that we all work in unison to produce great thinkers and leaders. We must all maintain an abundance of love for the children we lead, the subject matter for which we are responsible and *how* we actively involve the learner in ways that excite them. We all know the "Kevin's" and "Shane's" are coming. We must inspire and equip all learners and be proactive as we work alongside parents to prepare for the success of all scholars.

©MOVING MINDS™
www.moving-minds.com

MOVEMENT

*To change place or position; to advance

Movement is an absolute *must* in today's classroom. Erase all thoughts of desk in rows and students sitting around listening to a teacher. Those days are long gone! Today's students require movement as they study. Results observed in daily efforts as well as gains in test scores have proven this fact. Movement in the classroom creates a greater level of engagement and participation among all learners. Today's scholar is challenged to "go get" the lesson awaiting them. The student is now in control of his/her learning and the teacher has become a facilitator to help guide students towards their individual tasks and goals.

A decrease in the amount of discipline issues is a noted outcome when children can get out of their desks and move. Students are enjoying the activities involved with learning and do not want to miss out. Effective teachers know that children learn by doing and we plan daily/

weekly for activities to excite learners and keep them moving. We also know that most discipline issues arise from children whom are crying out for help. Allowing these students to move amongst their peers with respect for them, the classroom/teacher and all school expectations is only one piece of the puzzle. However, movement in the classroom must be thoughtfully planned and must be used regularly.

Math gallery walks involve displaying problems all around the classroom to practice and solve. Students are sent to work in small groups as the teacher can identify and address specific misconceptions. Once children have mastered certain concepts they become excited about the opportunity to show what they can do on their own. Movement in the classroom allows the teacher to assist a student privately without embarrassing them and encourages students to ask questions that they may not be comfortable asking in a whole group setting.

Presentations are another way we are getting scholars to move on a regular basis. As early as Kinder/1st grade students display an ability to speak and share ideas with their peers. This is the best way to deal with excessive talking in the classroom by students. Give them the stage and let them lead! The students are engaged, the presenter gets to educate and entertain, and the teacher is an active participant assisting leaders in the proper way to speak and address the audience. It's a win-win for us all!

> "Studies show that children who are more active exhibit better focus, faster cognitive processing, and more successful memory retention than kids who spend the day sitting still. Keeping the body active promotes mental clarity by increasing blood flow to the brain, making activity vital to both learning and physical and neurological health."
>
> – **Marwa Abdelbary**,
> Education Week, August 9, 2017.

Teachers have known this for some time. We all have been provided the tools to make the classroom a great place to explore and take chances. The question every parent must ask; "Is this happening regularly for my child and if it is not, Why?" Professional development courses guide teachers through proven strategies that excite learners and rid the classroom of boredom. No more sit and get…each student is an active participant in charge of their learning and it is their responsibility to address learning needs identified through collected data. The major role of the teacher has become to facilitate learners and guide them to proven methods and resources that make learning enjoyable.

As educators, we cannot ignore the lessons that children teach us. "I want to learn, but can I have fun while I do it?" Absolutely yes! Children who move in the classroom learn more through discovery and maintain knowledge gained for a longer period. Simply put, they are actively engaged for longer periods of time. This leads to learning that is cemented through mastery and this is the goal…not to pass a test. Today's teachers use movement regularly to keep students focused and this would be a great activity for parents to practice at home as well.

Copy the homework, cut it into parts, tape work to different areas of the home and attack problem solving situations as a family using all available resources. Take your time, use all strategies taught, stay level-headed and take breaks from problem solving to let the mind rest. Parents you will be amazed at how well your children can think on their feet!

Movement is a part of today's child and this point was "brought home to me" by a dear friend and veteran educator. We discussed the instructional methods of the past and how classrooms were evolving over time. "My early reading development was attained in the day when the radio was the number one form of entertainment." Due to this fact she believes that her generation was filled with great listeners armed with outstanding imaginations. I enjoyed immensely her sharing stories of "countless evening at home with family surrounding the speakers to catch regular programming that demanded listening to enjoy." It made sense that children learning then would not have a problem with the "sit and get" methods of the past.

We went on to discuss the importance of schools adjusting instructional methods of children introduced to television and computers. Scholars were adapting to new ways of learning that involved a more visual approach. The classroom had to evolve to include additional images and screens to help the learner of the day "cement" the knowledge attained. The filmstrip became a method of educating children at this time all over the country and it was not long before parents and students alike witness a growth and abundance of televisions in the classroom.

The effective teacher has always done what was necessary to connect with learners at their current level and provide proven techniques and strategies that assure growth. So, what does this mean for today's learner and movement in the classroom? We have been taught as educators that today's learner has a shorter attention span than any learner in recent history. We have been taught that technological advances in entertainment have assisted in creating children that are accustomed to movement in the form of games/gaming systems. To plan for today's scholar and all that we now know makes sense! To ignore the data is to ignore the needs of many of today's scholars.

So, what does movement in the classroom look like, exactly?

On most days, Mr. Sterling's classroom appears to be a small office in any major city in America. Students are "sent" to designated areas of the classroom to discover the learning that our team has thoughtfully planned out. Of course, I could give my students an assignment that will satisfy my state's objectives and keep everyone in their seats for 30-40 minutes, but why?

Let's take a review page designed to help students prepare for an upcoming math test. A "Gallery Walk" will afford the students the opportunity to discover learning by visiting math problems attached to different parts of the classroom. So, instead of sitting for 30-40 minutes in a desk, the student is actively engaged in meaningful discussions about problem solving as they navigate through a series of questions. The students support one another as strategies are shared and misconceptions are addressed. The fact that they are out of their seats makes all the difference in the world!

We still provide the scholar all the wonderful subject matter you know and love from your own educational background. We have only changed our methods of delivery to satisfy the needs of the learner. Not to worry, seats are provided, but they are optional. The student in today's classroom is completely engaged and responsible for their own learning and the teacher now plays the role of facilitator, used as a manager and resource if students need assistance. We know today's learner must move and educator's have made noted growth in achievement and engagement using simple techniques getting children out of their desks.

So how might this movement look in action? Imagine if you will… the common daily tasks a Math teacher may implement starting with HW review. Applying movement of small groups to review HW can give the instructor a truer sense of the level of mastery each student has achieved. No longer can students hide in the back and nod as if they understand. Now these students have expectations of meeting with the teacher daily to discuss details of the HW and which parts may have been most challenging. This can only happen efficiently if students can move in rotation.

While meeting with each small group, the remainder of the students will be completing related math tasks such as Daily Facts, Problem of the Day, Data/Graphs, Geometry and Technology-rich learning. This movement can be applied to Reading/Language Arts as well. Areas such as Phonemic Awareness, Vocabulary Review, Technology Integration, Test Taking Strategies, and Guided Reading will ensure that students are engaged in the learning process. Today's scholar is expected to track their own data and mastery levels, so teachers should be facilitating learners through a prescriptive routine where they can move about attacking their growth opportunities daily. The students are given a "preview" of each area along with classroom norms and expectations regarding time and effort. They are assigned their starting positions as small groups and sent to complete the days tasks in support of one another. I know can be a timekeeper and active assistant to the groups that require the most direct instruction.

Movement in the classroom is a must. Children should no longer be asked, in any classroom, to sit all day and learn. Tasks can simply be strategically placed throughout the learning environment to increase the level of student engagement. This will of course lead to higher levels of student achievement. Children are enjoying the learning process and parents, teachers, and school administrators are enjoying the outcomes today's engaged students are producing. Movement in the classroom also eliminates the quiet student "suffering in silence" because they are uncomfortable sharing shortcomings in front of their peers in a whole group setting. Guided small groups being able to move through planned tasks is vital to clearing student misconceptions and allows the student to work with confidence as they master the content and the process.

The length of time a student requires to complete tasks can vary depending on individual student needs. Every 8-15 minutes students physically go to different areas of the classroom to explore learning opportunities and discover knowledge that is both personal and meaningful to learner. Children can work at a comfortable pace and take ownership of their current levels of mastery. When the time ends, the small groups will come back together as a whole group to address student needs or questions.

There is no comparing a classroom that plans for daily movement versus one that keeps children sitting in their desks. The increased levels of engagement and interest are astonishing, and students, parents, and teachers are amazed by the volume of work students can produce when time and structure are maximized. The auditory, visual, and kinesthetic learner are all having their needs addressed and everyone is growing. Thoughtful grouping must also be considered to ensure focus as children move throughout the classroom. Movement will eliminate most, or all, discipline issues if used consistently. Bottom line, because they can move, children are having fun learning and the teacher has discovered a way to teach smarter and not harder!

Learning Station Set-Up Ideas

SUPPLY BUCKETS:
Place student supplies for each station to keep things organized and easy clean-up

DIRECTIONS & MODELS:
Include directions and models on each table so that students know their expectations for each learning station.

CENTERS/STATIONS

*Area of learning through discovery; area
where a student may complete a given task(s)
w/ materials and resources provided

Centers and stations are a change in today's classroom that many parents may be unaware of. Many of us simply did not experience learning at school this way. They play a vital role in the movement discussed previously. Centers and stations are areas of the classroom designed to advance young scholars through challenging tasks to be completed. They are most effective when properly planned, meet each learner where they are currently, and challenge the student to advance gradually at their own pace.

Centers and stations may be arranged by subject matter or themes based on daily or weekly lessons. In Math, for instance, the teacher may have areas set up for Whole Number Operations, Decimal Operations, Fractions, Measurement, Geometry, etc. In Reading/Language Arts a teacher may create areas of study dedicated to Reading Comprehension, Language Development, Writing Development, etc. Children are now independent learners gaining invaluable experience problem solving with their peers. Students can engage, explore, discover and create with other learners. Effective centers allow for student choice and increase student engagement and confidence through routines that target growth opportunities. The teacher is responsible for providing Centers/Stations that provide relevant activities intended to target weaknesses and transform them into strengths.

There is no right or wrong way to set up areas of study in the classroom, however, there are some constants that should apply across all Centers/Stations. First, data must lead the instruction! My students are required to take a diagnostic math test the first week of school. This exam will give me immediate feedback regarding each students' level of mastery in math from the previous school year. That information gives me the initial "areas" that must be addressed. As previously stated, today's learning is prescriptive, and Centers/Stations can be designed to meet learners where they are.

Secondly, Centers/Stations must provide materials and resources necessary to complete all given tasks. Ideally, the teacher can provide activities that address all types of learners.

- *Auditory (Listeners)
- *Visual (Sight)
- *Kinesthetic (Hands-on)

If a student is expected to measure, there should be rulers available for them to do so. If a science investigation is the expectation, it is a must that students are provided the tools to complete the job.

Third, technology must be accessible for learners as they complete tasks independently at Centers/Stations. Available technology will ensure that young scholars are engaged and excited about the opportunities to deepen their understanding of the subject matter. Technology apps/sites will also provide platforms for students to collaborate and provide feedback to peers. The resources online are endless, so without support and direction, a student could be overwhelmed by too many learning opportunities.

Students can now attain valuable independent/small group practice studying topics and objectives designed to increase student achievement. All small group Centers/Stations should be previewed in a whole group setting so that expectations are clear to the learner. Students will collect information regarding mastery of objectives in data binders that will guide them through required Centers/Stations. Students are showing a new level of excitement as they support one another and complete tasks together.

The teacher is afforded additional time and freedom to provide direct instruction to those students that require more attention.

It is not a simple transition for teachers to hand over the responsibility of learning to the student, but it is a decision I am more and more grateful I made every day. Most educators were taught in teacher-centered classrooms, yet today's classroom is one that is student-centered. Educator's today must give the responsibility of learning to the learner. It is their education and I will go as far as to say they want to be in control with the support of the teacher. Addressing weaknesses in the comfort of a small group at a Center/Station area is a welcomed relief for many students.

I also noticed that as students worked from station to station they showed a greater attention to detail. There was a noted increase in focus and many distractions I observed before going the route of Centers/Stations were gone. Student learning has become more organized and purposeful. It was clear that the children were finding comfort in the daily routine. Children learn by doing and Centers/Stations provide learners an intimate area to achieve mastery. They help students "cement" information introduced in whole group settings.

There appears to be no limit when it comes to the creativity that can go into student Centers/Stations. Effective educators, with the help of the scholars, create places where children feel free to explore without shame and discover new information that they will soon connect with their own background information. Students are in relaxed environments that have been proven to greatly increase academic gains as well as dramatically decreasing off-task behavior. Children are focused on the tasks at hand and are guided to success through rigorous routines that enhance learning at all levels and al learning styles. Along with displaying their own creative thoughts at Centers/Stations, students are afforded opportunities to attain critical social skills as they learn, share, and support other students in class.

Teachers are provided intimate daily/weekly "meetings" that help them truly know their students' weaknesses. Centers and Stations are then designed to meet those very needs by strengthening areas identified by student guided/independent practice. Parents must work in partnership with teachers to truly understand how their children learn best. We need parents to assist and support this instruction at home as well. Why not set up stations during HW time? We need parents to discuss these new age ways of learning with children and talk about how today's classroom compares to more "traditional" models of learning. The days of leaving students to "sit and get" for hours upon hours have come and gone. So, I would imagine trying to work for hours at home without a break would also prove to be less effective.

The children have shared on numerous occasions how much more they prefer this style of learning versus listening to someone talk for way too long. They want to have ownership of their learning and they appreciate a clear path to mastery. Is there evidence of Stations and/or Centers in your child's classroom? How will the teacher of record address identified weaknesses and reteach? Will there be activities and tasks in place for children who may be slightly above grade level? All of these questions, and more, can be answered with well thought out data driven Centers and Stations.

CENTERS/STATIONS SAMPLES BY SUBJECT

- Math – Task cards (data driven), pencils, dry erase markers and whiteboards, manipulatives, reference charts, multiplication chart, place value chart, problem solving expectations, released standardized tests, and technology
- Reading – Task cards (data driven), age appropriate library, magazines, newspaper, poetry, fiction, non-fiction, games/puzzles, parts of speech chart, expectations for reading: enjoyment versus information, and technology
- Science – Task cards (data driven), safety gear, measuring devices, timers, charts to collect data, solids,

liquids, gases, circuits, mirrors, Earth Sun and Moon models, games, puzzles, and technology
- Social Studies – Task cards (data driven), maps/globes, coloring pencils, coloring pages, appropriate literature, talking points, and technology

** Technology can be dispersed throughout
or centralized in one area.

TECHNOLOGY

*The study of applied sciences and engineering
*The practical application of knowledge

Today's classroom, just like most other places, are loaded with technology and parents must be aware of the amazing things students are doing regularly. Technology, such as, computers, laptops, cell phones, interactive learning sites and smart boards are all vital parts of keeping today's learner engaged in the process of attaining mastery. Today's parent must connect with educators and develop routines at home that mirror the use of technology being used at school. It is an ever changing and fast paced industry but not knowing what our children/students are exposed to regularly through technology can prove to be harmful.

As the parent, you have a right and duty to ensure your child is receiving an adequate amount of technology daily and weekly at school. This technology should be readily available, and all students should be instructed on proper usage. Teachers must plan daily and weekly lessons integrating technology throughout. Many sites visited regularly by educators keep children engaged and provide different perspectives to any topic of study. Most learners appreciate the opportunities to deepen their understanding of an objective through games, interactive labs, virtual vocabulary and too many others to go on. We know children learn by doing and technology in today's classroom is taking our scholars to new and unknown realities. Imagine creating power point presentations or practicing virtual back surgery in elementary school! Technology is making learning fun and all parties involved are excited about that! Once, the parent and teacher become one force and many of the sites visited in school are mirrored in the home, amazing growth happens!

Our daily announcements began each day with a live video feed from our principal as she addresses the entire school. She is joined by Journalism Club students whom assist with daily important information shared through classroom "smart boards".

After the announcements have concluded, I began to share the days Learning Expectations and Success Criteria by projecting power point slides to communicate the days agenda. Student laptops are then passed out to assist learners with growth opportunities identified through collected data. We play games, sing songs and complete interactive labs all designed to strengthen areas using engaging technology. The students have spoken… they love learning this way!

The online resources available to teachers and scholars today are limitless and can bring to life any topic being studied. I will share some of my favorites and give a brief description of each and how they have personally assisted me with keeping children excited about learning. The magic happens when technology allows learning to be prescriptive. Technology, applied properly, affords us the opportunities to differentiate learning and meet all scholars at their current levels of comprehension and skills. We can now advance the learner with a regular and comfortable routine as they work at their own pace.

Flocabulary.com was created to assist learners' vocabulary mastery through song while "increasing academic achievement and fostering a love of learning in every student". This a paid site and it is worth every red cent invested! Flocabulary.com meets state standards through vocabulary instruction ranging from Kindergarten to SAT test prep for high school students. Students can study a variety of subjects such as Vocabulary, Math, Science, Language Arts, Life Skills, Social Studies, and Current Events.

Along with amazing music and well thought out lyrics, Flocabulary offers for each lesson a video, vocabulary cards, vocabulary game, read and respond activity, quiz and a lyric lab providing a platform for creativity. You will also find additional resources and printable activities with answer keys provided. Flocabulary has become an essential tool in today's classroom and is creating amazing growth for today's learners when used routinely. "On average, students using Flocabulary.com scored 25% higher on state reading tests".

Brainpop.com, created in 1999, was founded "as a creative way to explain difficult concepts". Today it is "a trusted learning resource supporting core and supplemental subjects, reaching millions of learners worldwide". Brainpop provides learners an interactive experience with a 3-6-minute cartoon video lesson as an anchor. The characters are engaging and informative. Scholars also have access to related quizzes, activities, related reading and games. They can even create their own movie with "Make a Movie". This tool "empowers students and teachers to make their own BrainPOP-style movies. Simply choose a topic, build scenes using BrainPOP images and animations or draw your own, then add narration".

I have used Brainpop.com for my entire teaching career and it has never let me down. Over the years, I have shared this site with parents and the overwhelming response has always been one of pure joy in seeing their children engaged and excited about learning. The topics include Science, Social Studies, English, Math, Arts/Music, Health, Engineering/Technology, and New/Trending. As students identify growth opportunities, they can access Brainpop.com, in whole or small group settings, to attack and transform weaknesses into strengths! With topics ranging from elementary to secondary instruction, I submit this site should be a part of any scholar's educational routine.

Khanacademy.org literally offers "a free world class education to anyone, anywhere"! This sight is a must for the classroom and study at home. We are currently moving into the world of "Blended Learning", an approach to education that combines online educational materials and opportunities for interaction online with traditional place-based classroom methods. It requires the physical presence of both teacher and student, with some elements of student control over time, place, path, or pace. (Wikipedia, 2019)

> "Khan Academy offers practice exercises, instructional videos, and a personalized learning dashboard that empower learners to study at their own pace in and outside of the classroom. We tackle math, science, computer programming, history, art history, economics, and more. Our math missions guide learners from kindergarten to calculus using state-of-the-art, adaptive technology that identifies strengths and learning gaps."
>
> – Khanacademy.org

I am quite pleased to share learning websites and technology with students and parents. To see excited learners, discover knowledge regularly through new and innovative resources excites me as an educator. Technology must be applied routinely in today's classroom to connect with and engage young scholars. Today's classroom instruction must be informative and interesting for all involved. The level of student engagement when learning with technology is unrivaled. It is simply the world our students live in and it would be foolish of us not to use technology regularly as we educate.

Students are offered an intimate relationship with the knowledge they seek out and attain. They connect for longer periods of time while studying with technology and gain a deeper level of comprehension through problem solving. The information students get is personal and moves beyond the short-term memory to a place where learning can be felt. Children using technology as they learn are joyous and they are singing, dancing, and laughing as they work! When there is a focus on the regular use of technology, and its immeasurable opportunities in today's classroom, amazing learning and growth happens. The classroom has a relaxed atmosphere and students are exploring without fear of shame or ridicule. Technology has changed the way we teach today and how students learn. Inquire yearly the sites and activities being utilized in the classroom that enhance your child's education through technology. Be there to support them and watch them soar to new heights.

*NOTABLE SITES (MUST!)

- Studyjams.com (Math/Science) k-8
- Interactivesites.weebly.com (All Subjects/ Early Childhood)
- Starfall.com (Reading/Early Childhood)
- K-5 Math Resources.com
- Education Galaxy.com (Adaptive Intervention)
- Prodigy.com (Gr1-8) Math Mastery
- Khanacademy.org (Math/Science)
- Flocabulary.com (All Subjects K-12)

COOPERATIVE LEARNING GROUPS

*Cooperate – to work together and
complete independent practice

Most of today's classroom instruction and guided practice is done in small productive learning groups. These groups may be homogeneous; "the placement of students of similar abilities into one small group". They may be heterogenous; "a type of distribution of students among various groups". Only during times of assessment are students asked to perform independently. One major goal of this method of instruction is to allow students the opportunities to discuss orally newly gained knowledge and skills while connecting the information to background knowledge already attained. Their learning is strengthened by chances provided daily to apply these new skills within a safe and respectful group of peer supporters.

Instructors from every grade level and across all subjects use group work to enhance their students' learning. Whether the goal is to increase student understanding of content, to build transferable skills, instructors often turn to small group work to capitalize on the benefits of peer-to-peer instruction. It is defined as "the instructional use of small groups to promote students working together to maximize their own and each other's learning". Cooperative learning is characterized by positive interdependence, where students perceive that better performance by individuals produces better performance by the entire group.

Learning becomes more meaningful for students working in cooperative learning groups. Recent studies also suggest that student knowledge and skills are maintained for longer periods of time as students are encouraged to casually engage in topics of study in relaxed and inviting atmospheres. Peers speak the same language and scholars assisting scholars is a "win-win" for all parties involved. The weaker student has constant support to address any misconceptions and the stronger student has any opportunity to strengthen their knowledge by instructing others. Students began to discover cooperatively the best ways to answer questions and/or solve problems.

"Think, Pair, & Share" is a very popular strategy used for instruction in today's classroom. Think of it as fuel for cooperative learning groups. Step 1 – Have four students in a small group think or write about a discussion question. Step 2 – Allow students to turn to a partner and discuss their responses. Step 3 – Start a whole group discussion by having each pair share their responses with the class. Students are now able to review their answer choices alongside peers and make changes if necessary. A well facilitated group can eliminate misconceptions before independent practice and maximize the time and effort that young scholars will invest in their quest for mastery.

Another favorite in today's classroom is the "Jigsaw" approach to cooperative learning groups. In this method, groups of students become "experts" on one segment of new material, while other teams become "experts" on other segments of new material. Next, the class is rearranged into new groups, having one expert from each team present to the class on their findings. The members of the new team then take turns teaching each other the material on which they are experts! The teacher of record has now become a facilitator and assist students with defining the learning objectives for the activity and assigning students to groups. Teachers should play an active role during the groups' work, monitoring the work and evaluating group and individual performance. Instructors also encourage groups to reflect on their interactions to identify potential improvements for future group work.

Effective classrooms today display children who are well behaved and extremely focused on the tasks at hand.

They are presented regularly with opportunities to share and express their own ideas, thoughts and opinions. With all the questioning opportunities in the classroom, it would be impossible for teachers to allow each student to speak independently for every question. However, if given the proper amount of time to share, all students can make valuable discoveries, and input, with cooperative learning groups. Children get excited about new information, as they should, and it is a must they are given opportunities to express their feelings and make real connections to the curriculum. The students learn to respect when the teacher is talking because they know that their time to talk and share is soon to come!

Through guided discussions, students in cooperative learning groups can take new information to deeper levels of comprehension. Students begin to discover proper use of time management and effective work strategies that ensure success. "Quick Checks", "Quick Writes" and major assessments provide feedback to today's learners and it is their responsibility to analyze data and strengthen areas identified as weaknesses. This information also assists in the design of cooperative learning groups. Students can have their educational needs met "prescriptively" in small groups without fear of ridicule or shame.

Today's classroom is designed to "catch" learners who may "fall through the cracks" and reteach them using a variety of techniques and resources. Small groups also meet the needs of scholars that may need to be challenged on a higher level. Educators must be wise in the groups we create and must constantly monitor and adjust them as necessary. Differentiation means tailoring instruction to meet individual needs. Therefore, cooperative learning groups is a must! We must provide support for learners that need additional time and practice to achieve mastery. We must also maintain the interest and engagement level of high achievers, ensuring that they are growing daily as well.

If your child is not exposed regularly to cooperative learning groups, you may want to ask why. We know that small groups benefit all learners in today's classroom. We know that learning becomes more meaningful when scholars can share and discuss new information as they connect it to background knowledge. We know that children learn best when they feel safe and empowered to try without fear of failure. We know that children are more likely to stay focused and on task when given the opportunity to work alongside peers. There are fewer distractions and discipline is transformed into self-discipline. Many of us understand that without the opportunity to share in cooperative learning groups, children may sometimes create their own opportunities to speak with or without permission.

In preparing students for cooperative learning groups, teachers must provide "learning intentions" and "success criteria" including social skills and academic expectations. Assigning group roles and rotating them regularly may halt issues with dominance or conflict. It is the role of the educator to monitor interactions, intervene to help students with problems, and assist in the completion of tasks while ensuring scholars are working together effectively. It is the role of the parent to work side by side with the teacher and attack identified weaknesses at home. It is the role of the student to work side by side with the teacher and attack identified weaknesses at school. Well designed cooperative learning groups plus effort equals success!

9 TIPS FOR
ORGANIZING
INTERACTIVE NOTEBOOKS
Lucky Little Learners

INTERACTIVE NOTE-BOOKING

*Interactive – allowing a two-way flow of information between input and output

One of the most important, exciting, and useful tools we use in today's classrooms are Interactive Notebooks. Students are excited to create a resource that bridges learning levels to ensure mastery. Teachers are excited for children to have a way to organize their thoughts and prepare for assessments. Parents are excited that they now have a resource that connects what scholars are doing at school to what their expectations may be at home. Students are asked to take ownership of their learning and interactive notebooks provide learners an opportunity to practice, reflect, and clear misconceptions in a guided format that will ensure growth. No longer are assignments disregarded, but this evidence of knowledge gained is stapled or glued chronologically throughout the school year serving as an ongoing journal.

Interactive notebooks provide students an opportunity to take teacher provided notes, respond creatively through writing or art, and express themselves routinely as they connect background knowledge to new information gained. The notebooks become year long projects that allow learners to organize their thinking. Routing processes such as daily page numbers, titles, table of contents, and choice of input/output ideas build structure in educational development. Students that are provided systems for organization perform better in and out of class than those without a system.

Interactive notebooks assist tremendously towards bridging any gaps they may exists from in class learning and support to homework and additional support. These notebooks become a resource that parents can use to "take a peek" into the classroom. Daily students are asked to title each page and date the assignment to be completed. They record what we call "I do, We do, You do!" inside their notebooks. Today's student is also responsible for recording daily "learning intentions and success criteria". Organization and routine become the norm and scholars grow daily in confidence. Misconceptions are addressed immediately as students can explore and learn through discovery. Along with peer observation and feedback, note-booking becomes an amazing tool for transforming weaknesses into strengths.

Note-booking encourages the learner to become resourceful and apply knowledge gained in problem solving situations. The student is constantly forced to refer to guided whole group and small group mini-lessons previously recorded. Scholars begin to attain mastery through the process of self-reflection and peer feedback as they record each step along the way. Ultimately, each student is creating a personal portfolio of their own development. Students reflect upon their efforts and think about new information used to deepen their comprehension and mastery of an objective. Content is ordered and simple to reference. Educators also use Interactive Notebooks to differentiate learning and provide a "prescriptive" approach to achievement. Today's learner can keep a record of new information, their personal responses and attempts to problem solve, as well as, feedback provided to increase achievement and mastery.

INTERACTIVE NOTE-BOOKING MUST!

1. Table of Contents! – Students must date daily efforts and provide a title. Learning intentions and success criteria are optional depending on age and ability.
2. Input/Output Ideas per subject:
    *   Math – Measurements Reference Guide, 100's chart/multiplication chart, problem solving model/expectations, place value/

- decimal place value chart, fraction bars, pre-assessments/rubric and goals!
- Science – sentence stems, concept maps, personal experience connection, labeled drawings, acrostic poems, graphic organizer, questions/quick writes diagrams/graphs/tables, safety contracts, notebook expectations/rubric

3. Learned activities, fun and creativity!

BETTERLEARNING.COM

"Interactive notebooks allow leaders to record information and process it to gain a deeper level of understanding. As scholars learn new information, several types of writing and graphic techniques will be used to record this information." Students are expected to interact with learned information and apply critical thinking skills "to organize and process information." This my friends is where the "magic" of hard work, routines, and self-reflection begin to shape learners into scholars responsible for their own mastery!

"As a result, learners become more creative, more independent thinkers as well as gaining a deeper understanding of what they are learning and how they are learning."

BETTERLEARNING.COM "WE DO THIS BECAUSE"

1. Simply writing something down does not mean you have learned it.
2. A learner must become actively involved with information before they can truly understand it.
3. Scholars will organize and eventually learn to plan for ways to apply new learning.
4. Students are giving permission to be playful and creative in their responses without fear of 'messing up'
5. Educators must be reminded that students need time to absorb ideas as learning is introduced and applied.
6. Metacognition is the goal! Scholars thinking about their thinking.
7. This notebook becomes an amazing study tool for tests/state test and bridge to lessons waiting at the next grade level. It will teach children how to study!

"LEADER IN ME!"

It has been my honor and privilege to work at Holley E.S. with an amazing group of educators, administrators, teacher aides, cafeteria staff, custodial staff, and parent volunteers. We have been given the responsibility, and joy, of transforming students into leaders through the "Leader in Me!" program being taught through Stephen Covey's book *The 7 Habits of Highly Effective People (1989)*.

*Leader in me (online) Parent's Guide 2017

"You are your child's first and best teacher. You lay the foundation for education of your child's mind, heart, body, and spirit. No matter what's going on in your child's school, you can help your son or daughter discover the leader within and prepare for a great life of contribution and service."

HABIT 1 – BE PROACTIVE!

"You're in charge of yourself!"

"I have a can do attitude and always try my best at every-thing I do. I follow instructions and do the right things without being asked, even when nobody is looking. I choose my actions, attitudes and moods and don't blame others for my wrongdoing."

HABIT 2 – BEGIN WITH THE END IN MIND

"Have a Plan!"

"I plan ahead and set goals for myself. I am prepared at all times. I think about how the choices I make now will affect my future. I think about the positive or negative consequences of my actions before I act."

HABIT 3 – PUT FIRST THINGS FIRST

"Work first, then play!"

"I do the things that I have to do before I do the things that I want to do. I stay focused on what I'm doing. I try to minimize distractions and regroup if I get off task. I spend my time on things that are the most important."

HABIT 4 – THINK WIN-WIN

"Everybody can win!"

"I can problem solve when an issue comes up with another person. I think about what other people want and not just what I want. I am kind to others and try to think of ways to help everyone to be happy."

HABIT 5 – SEEK FIRST TO UNDERSTAND, THEN TO BE UNDERSTOOD

"Listen before you speak!"

"I listen to others without interrupting. I raise my hand when I want to speak and I wait to be called on. I don't blurt out. I try to understand other people's views and feelings, even if they are different from my own."

HABIT 6 – SYNERGIZE

"Working together is better!"

"I get along well with other people and work well in groups. I value the strengths of others and allow myself to learn from them. I know that by working together as a team we can get more done and come up with better solutions than we could alone."

HABIT 7 – SHARPEN THE SAW

"Balance is best!"

"I take care of my body by eating right, exercising, and getting enough sleep. I balance my time between school, extracurricular activities, family, and friends. I am always learning how to become a better person."

The 7 Habits have been truly transformational in every regard. Every member of our school community has been invited, sometimes reluctantly, to take a long and endearing look in the mirror. From this sincere exercise in ethics and integrity, and sometimes insecurity and fear, have abounded amazing leaders in every position from principals/asst. principals to teachers/teacher aides to parents/students. My students often hear me remind them, "The most growth happens when we are honest about our weaknesses and view them as growth opportunities." The 7 Habits provide students a safe place to learn, reflect and share/receive peer feedback to assist in the development of all learners.

The following topics are tools utilized regularly by parents and teachers alike to transform the lives of children. "Leader in Me" schools and districts are providing amazing support to both home and school communities and "Today's Parent!" must know about "today's classroom".

- *Getting Involved at School
- *Importance of Goals
- *Organizational Skills
- *Family Mission Statements
- *Supporting "Leader in Me!"
- *Readers are Leaders
- *Community Volunteerism
- *Leadership Roles at Home
- *Respecting Diversity

5E INSTRUCTIONAL METHOD!

*Today's learning/teaching model for today's classroom

The 5E Instructional Model is utilized daily in today's classroom and is an important tool for ensuring that the learner's mastery of content remains the major focus for every lesson provided. Many schools/districts today are even requiring educators to share daily Learning Intentions and Success Criteria so it obvious to all scholars "why" they are learning, "what" they are learning, as well as "how" they will master the content.

ENGAGE – The purpose of the Engage stage is to capture student interest and assist them in developing a guiding question that the student will discover through exploration. The student should be invited to become personally involved in the lesson and the teacher is afforded an opportunity to "pre-assess" student background knowledge.

EXPLORE – During the Explore stage of the lesson the student is now asked to physically, interactively and/or mentally manipulate activities designed to help the learner build their own understanding of the content. The teacher may guide learners at this stage to focus on the "big idea" and help them "see" or visualize where the lesson is going.

EXPLAIN – The purpose for the Explain stage is to provide scholars an opportunity to communicate what they have learned so far and begin to figure out what it means. Now we ask…"What questions or techniques will help the student connect their explore activities to the concept being studied?" Educators can now present higher order thinking questions designed to collect student responses and help them justify their explanations.

ELABORATE/EXTEND – The purpose for the Elaborate/Extend stage is to allow scholars the opportunity to apply new knowledge and continue to explore the topic at a deeper level. Teachers may introduce or review daily vocabulary terms and help the learner connect meaning to student observations. This is also the stage where the student can answer, "How is this knowledge applied in my daily life?"

EVALUATE – The purpose of the Evaluate stage is for both the student and the teacher to determine how much learning and understanding has taken place. At his stage students should be ready to demonstrate that they have mastered the lesson objective. Quick checks for student understanding should be given throughout the lesson, as well as in conclusion.

CONCLUSION

In conclusion, I would like to thank each and every reader for investing time and effort in this book. The very fabric of learning through discovery is joy and exploration. This joy should be experienced by all learners and all children can love learning and grow. Today's classroom is offering today's students an opportunity to learn in a fashion that is both engaging and empowering to the learner. The student is taking ownership of their learning and honest intervention based on student data is leading the way. No longer are we starting at page 1 and working to page 350. Today's classroom is prescriptive! We are identifying areas of growth to be strengthened and maximizing the efforts of all involved to benefit the scholar.

The responsibility of educating today's child "must" belong to us all. They are the future and they need us to guide, facilitate, and empower them through a world that is sometimes very unkind. Again, I don't claim to have all the answers, but I do have a record of student growth that speaks to the joy, passion and effort I put into every "must" discussed in this book. I know how precious every child is that is entrusted to my care and I know how much they mean to every parent that I meet. Parents must work in partnership with teachers and only then can the best plan for every child be created and executed properly. Teachers must understand how to work "smarter not harder". Our role has been transformed to facilitator and guiding students to find the greatness within should be our ultimate goal.

Bottom line, the child and family will get what they put in when it comes to education. Real growth and change takes time and a consistent routine with clear expectations. My goal is to inform and empower parents. You should know the opportunities available to today's learners and how excited children get for the chance to engage with technology and other modes of instruction. Parents should also be aware of growth opportunities identified and must be on board when it comes to attacking weak areas. It truly takes a village to raise a child. I believe what we are seeing, in too many of today's schools, is a direct result of a disconnect between the parent and the teacher. Somehow, we went from being admired to being ridiculed and no longer trusted. Unfortunately, the best of us do not get the coverage that the worst of us receives. My goal again, is to bridge that gap. Today's best teaching methods can no longer be ignored and today's parent can ensure that their child/children are getting a highly effective educator in every classroom.

Today's classroom is all about the student and if the school of choice for your child does not give that very particular energy, questions should be raised as to why. Why am I unaware of the technology usage available to my child daily/weekly and the programs available for the home? Why am I unaware of the amount of movement available to my child as they learn? Why am I unaware of what station and centers are utilized to attack identified weaknesses? Why am I unaware of today's expectation for my child to "work well with others" in cooperative learning groups? Why am I unaware of the importance of interactive note booking and how it prepares my child for the next level of instruction? Why do I not have a sincere professional relationship with an individual that spends hundreds of hours instructing my child? It is time to collectively answer these questions and more.

Today's classroom is transformational! We truly can't afford to leave any child behind. The cost is too great. I'll conclude with our classroom mission statement read daily by all scholars. Please share this text if it can be of benefit to a parent or student.

"Our mission is to *work hard* together
each day and *maximize* our *potential*
to be great leaders and citizens!"

* 9 7 8 1 6 3 8 3 7 6 9 9 6 *